The Poetry Of Robert Nichols
Volume 1 – Ardours & Endurances

Robert Malise Bowyer Nichols was born in September 1893.

Robert was educated at Winchester College and then Trinity College, Oxford. In September 1914 with the shadow of the Great War covering Europe he enlisted, despite poor health, with the Field Artillery. He trained for a year and reached the front line just before the beginning of the Battle of Loos in September 1915. He was also to serve at the Battle of the Somme as an artillery officer in 1916, after suffering from shell shock he was invalided back to England.

Taking up service with The British Ministry of Labour and the Ministry of Information he began to write more avidly. As one of the War's surviving poets he was able to also give his work a depth and reflection that many of his other fallen contemporaries were not able too. He also began to give readings of his poems as well as tours in America.

Robert also wrote four plays and two novels as well as several further volumes of poetry. Now rightly regarded as one of the pre-eminent War Poets his poetry is richly rewarding, filled with vivid descriptions and emotions of the human suffering during war.

It's end brought him together with Nancy Cunard who was the inspiration for his next book Aurelia (1920). He was in Tokyo from 1921 to 1924 teaching English Literature and from 1924 to 1926 Hollywood beckoned.

In 1928 his play, Wings Over Europe, foretelling the splitting of the atom was a success in New York. In 1933-4 he was in Austria and Germany, his long weekly letters to Henry Head, the neurologist under whose care he had been for shell-shock, give a graphic eye-witness account of the rise of Hitler.

By the end of the 1930's he was living in the South of France, his emotional and financial affairs in turmoil. With occupation of France by German and Vichy forces he was on the last ship to carry British refugees from the Cote d'Azur.

Robert Nichols died on December 17th 1944. He is buried at St Mary's, in Lawford, Essex.

Index Of Poems

I. In the Grass: Halt by Roadside
II. The Day's March
III. Nearer

BATTLE:
I. Noon
II. Night Bombardment
III. Comrades: An Episode
IV. Behind the Lines: Night, France
V. At the Wars
VI. Out of Trenches: The Barn, Twilight
VII. Battery moving up to a New Position from Rest Camp: Dawn
VIII. Eve of Assault: Infantry going down to Trenches
IX. The Assault
X. The Last Morning
XI. Fulfilment

THE DEAD:
I. The Burial in Flanders
II. Boy
III. Plaint of Friendship by Death Broken
IV. By the Wood

THE AFTERMATH:
I. At the Ebb
II. Alone
III. Thanksgiving
IV. Annihilated
V. Shut of Night
VI. The Full Heart
VII. Sonnet: Our Dead
VIII. Deliverance

OTHER POEMS:
Address To The Sunset
Evenstar
Farewell
Fulfilment
I Must Remember Now
Nearer
Night Rhapsody
November
O Nightingale My Heart
PÆan
Seventeen
The Flower Of Flame
The Last Salute
The Pilgrim
The Sprig of Lime
The Stranger
The Tower

1. Of The Nature Of The Poet:

"We are (often) so impressed by the power of poetry that we think of it as something made by a wonderful and unusual person: we do not realize the fact that all the wonder and marvel is in our own brains, that the poet is ourselves. He speaks our language better than we do merely because he is more skilful with it than we are; his skill is part of our skill, his power of our power; generations of English-speaking men and women have made us sensible to these things, and our sensibility comes from the same source that the poet's power of stimulating it comes from.

Given a little more sensitiveness to external stimuli, a little more power of associating ideas, a co-ordination of the functions of expression somewhat more apt, a sense of rhythm somewhat keener than the average, given these things we should be poets, too, even as he is.... He is one of us."

2. Of What English Poetry Consists:

"English poetry is not a rhythm of sound, but a rhythm of ideas, and the flow of attention-stresses (i.e., varying qualities of words and cadence) which determines its beauty is inseparably connected with the thought; for each of them is a judgment of identity, or a judgment of relation, or an expression of relation, and not a thing of mere empty sound.... He who would think of it as a pleasing arrangement of vocal sounds has missed all chance of ever understanding its meaning. There awaits him only the barren generalities of a foreign prosody, tedious, pedantic, fruitless. And he will flounder ceaselessly amid the scattered timbers of its iambuses, spondees, dactyls, tribrachs, never reaching the firm ground of truth."

"AN INTRODUCTION TO THE SCIENTIFIC STUDY OF ENGLISH POETRY,"[1] by MARK LIDDELL.

[1] Published by Grant Richards (1902). This remarkable book, establishing English poetry as a thing governed from within by its own necessities, and not by rules of æsthetics imposed on it from without, formulates principles which, unperceived, have governed English poetry from the earliest times, which find their greatest exemplar in Shakespeare, and which, though beginning to be realized by the less pedantic of the moderns, are in its pages for the first time lucidly expounded And, such is their adequacy, can, in the end, only be regarded as indubitably proven. R. M. B. N., 1917.

ARDOURS AND ENDURANCES
TO THE MEMORY OF MY TRUSTY AND GALLANT FRIENDS:
HAROLD STUART GOUGH (King's Royal Rifle Corps)
AND RICHARD PINSENT (the Worcester Regiment)

"For what is life if measured by the space,
Not by the act?"
BEN JONSON.

THE SUMMONS

I. TO----
Asleep within the deadest hour of night
And, turning with the earth, I was aware
How suddenly the eastern curve was bright,
As when the sun arises from his lair.
But not the sun arose: it was thy hair
Shaken up heaven in tossing leagues of light.

Since then I know that neither night nor day
May I escape thee, O my heavenly hell!
Awake, in dreams, thou springest to waylay
And should I dare to die, I know full well
Whose voice would mock me in the mourning bell,
Whose face would greet me in hell's fiery way.

II. THE PAST
How to escape the bondage of the past?
I fly thee, yet my spirit finds no calms
Save when she deems her rocked within those arms
To which, from which she ne'er was caught or cast.

O sadness of a heart so spent in vain,
That drank its age's fuel in an hour:
For whom the whole world burning had not power
To quick with life the smouldered wick again!

III. THE RECKONING
The whole world burns, and with it burns my flesh.
Arise, thou spirit spent by sterile tears;
Thine eyes were ardent once, thy looks were fresh,
Thy brow shone bright amid thy shining peers.
Fame calls thee not, thou who hast vainly strayed
So far for her; nor Passion, who in the past
Gave thee her ghost to wed and to be paid;
Nor Love, whose anguish only learned to last.

Honour it is that calls: canst thou forget

Once thou wert strong? Listen; the solemn call
Sounds but this once again. Put by regret
For summons missed, or thou hast missed them all.
Body is ready, Fortune pleased; O let
Not the poor Past cost the proud Future's fall.

FAREWELL TO PLACE OF COMFORT

For the last time, maybe, upon the knoll
I stand. The eve is golden, languid, sad....
Day like a tragic actor plays his role
To the last whispered word, and falls gold-clad.
I, too, take leave of all I ever had.

They shall not say I went with heavy heart:
Heavy I am, but soon I shall be free;
I love them all, but O I now depart
A little sadly, strangely, fearfully,
As one who goes to try a Mystery.

The bell is sounding down in Dedham Vale:
Be still, O bell! too often standing here
When all the air was tremulous, fine, and pale,
Thy golden note so calm, so still, so clear,
Out of my stony heart has struck a tear.

And now tears are not mine. I have release
From all the former and the later pain;
Like the mid-sea I rock in boundless peace,
Soothed by the charity of the deep sea rain....
Calm rain! Calm sea! Calm found, long sought in vain.

O bronzen pines, evening of gold and blue,
Steep mellow slope, brimmed twilit pools below,
Hushed trees, still vale dissolving in the dew,
Farewell! Farewell! There is no more to do.
We have been happy. Happy now I go.

THE APPROACH

I. IN THE GRASS: HALT BY ROADSIDE

In my tired, helpless body
I feel my sunk heart ache;
But suddenly, loudly
The far, the great guns shake.

Is it sudden terror

Burdens my heart? My hand
Flies to my head. I listen....
And do not understand.

Is death so near, then?
From this blaze of light
Do I plunge suddenly
Into Vortex? Night?

Guns again! the quiet
Shakes at the vengeful voice....
It is terrible pleasure.
I do not fear: I rejoice.

II. THE DAY'S MARCH

The battery grides and jingles,
Mile succeeds to mile;
Shaking the noonday sunshine,
The guns lunge out awhile,
And then are still awhile.

We amble along the highway;
The reeking, powdery dust
Ascends and cakes our faces
With a striped, sweaty crust.

Under the still sky's violet
The heat thróbs on the air....
The white road's dusty radiance
Assumes a dark glare.

With a head hot and heavy,
And eyes that cannot rest,
And a black heart burning
In a stifled breast,

I sit in the saddle,
I feel the road unroll,
And keep my senses straightened
Toward to-morrow's goal.

There, over unknown meadows
Which we must reach at last,
Day and night thunders
A black and chilly blast.

Heads forget heaviness,
Hearts forget spleen,
For by that mighty winnowing
Being is blown clean.

Light in the eyes again,
Strength in the hand,
A spirit dares, dies, forgives,
And can understand!

And, best! Love comes back again
After grief and shame,
And along the wind of death
Throws a clean flame.

The battery grides and jingles,
Mile succeeds to mile;
Suddenly battering the silence
The guns burst out awhile.

I lift my head and smile.

III. NEARER
Nearer and ever nearer....
My body, tired but tense,
Hovers 'twixt vague pleasure
And tremulous confidence.

Arms to have and to use them
And a soul to be made
Worthy if not worthy;
If afraid, unafraid.

To endure for a little,
To endure and have done:
Men I love about me,
Over me the sun!

And should at last suddenly
Fly the speeding death,
The four great quarters of heaven
Receive this little breath.

BATTLE

I. NOON
It is midday: the deep trench glares....
A buzz and blaze of flies....
The hot wind puffs the giddy airs....
The great sun rakes the skies.

No sound in all the stagnant trench
Where forty standing men

Endure the sweat and grit and stench,
Like cattle in a pen.

Sometimes a sniper's bullet whirs
Or twangs the whining wire;
Sometimes a soldier sighs and stirs
As in hell's frying fire.

From out a high cool cloud descends
An aeroplane's far moan....
The sun strikes down, the thin cloud rends....
The black speck travels on.

And sweating, dizzied, isolate
In the hot trench beneath,
We bide the next shrewd move of fate
Be it of life or death.

II. NIGHT BOMBARDMENT

Softly in the silence the evening rain descends....
The soft wind lifts the rain-mist, flurries it, and spends
Its grief in mournful sighs, drifting from field to field,
Soaking the draggled sprays which the low hedges wield
As they labour in the wet and the load of the wind.
The last light is dimming; night comes on behind.

I hear no sound but the wind and the rain,
And trample of horses, loud and lost again
Where the waggons in the mist rumble dimly on
Bringing more shell.
The last gleam is gone.
It is not day or night; only the mists unroll
And blind with their sorrow the sight of my soul.

I hear the wind weeping in the hollow overhead:
She goes searching for the forgotten dead
Hidden in the hedges or trodden into muck
Under the trenches, or maybe limply stuck
Somewhere in the branches of a high lonely tree
He was a sniper once. They never found his body.

I see the mist drifting. I hear the wind and rain,
And on my clammy face the oozed breath of the slain
Seems to be blowing. Almost I have heard
In the shuddering drift the lost dead's last word:

Go home, go home, go to my house;
Knock at the door, knock hard, arouse
My wife and the children, that you must do
What do you say? Tell the children, too

Knock at the door, knock hard, arouse
The living. Say: the dead won't come back to this house.
O ... but it's cold, I soak in the rain
Shrapnel found me, I shan't come home again
No, not home again!

The mourning voices trail
Away into rain, into darkness ... the pale
Soughing of the night drifts on in between.

The Voices were as if the dead had never been.

O melancholy heavens, O melancholy fields,
The glad, full darkness grows complete and shields
Me from your appeal.
With a terrible delight
I hear far guns low like oxen at the night.
Flames disrupt the sky.
The work is begun.
"Action!" My guns crash, flame, rock and stun
Again and again. Soon the soughing night
Is loud with their clamour and leaps with their light.

The imperative chorus rises sonorous and fell:
My heart glows lighted as by fires of hell.
Sharply I pass the terse orders down.
The guns blare and rock. The hissing rain is blown
Athwart the hurtled shell that shrilling, shrilling goes
Away into the dark, to burst a cloud of rose
Over German trenches.
A pause: I stand and see
Lifting into the night like founts incessantly
The pistol-lights' pale spores upon the glimmering air....
Under them furrowed trenches empty, pallid, bare....
And rain snowing trenchward ghostly and white.

O dead in the hedges, sleep ye well to-night!

III. COMRADES: AN EPISODE
Before, before he was aware
The 'Verey' light had risen ... on the air
It hung glistering....
And he could not stay his hand
From moving to the barbed wire's broken strand.
A rifle cracked.
He fell.
Night waned. He was alone. A heavy shell
Whispered itself passing high, high overhead.
His wound was wet to his hand: for still it bled
On to the glimmering ground.

Then with a slow, vain smile his wound he bound,
Knowing, of course, he'd not see home again
Home whose thought he put away.
His men
Whispered: "Where's Mister Gates?" "Out on the wire."
"I'll get him," said one....
Dawn blinked, and the fire
Of the Germans heaved up and down the line.
"Stand to!"
Too late! "I'll get him." "O the swine!
When we might get him in yet safe and whole!"
"Corporal didn't see 'un fall out on patrol,
Or he'd 'a got 'un." "Sssh!"
"No talking there."
A whisper: "'A went down at the last flare."
Meanwhile the Maxims toc-toc-tocked; their swish
Of bullets told death lurked against the wish.
No hope for him!
His corporal, as one shamed,
Vainly and helplessly his ill-luck blamed.

Then Gates slowly saw the morn
Break in a rosy peace through the lone thorn
By which he lay, and felt the dawn-wind pass
Whispering through the pallid, stalky grass
Of No-Man's Land....
And the tears came
Scaldingly sweet, more lovely than a flame.
He closed his eyes: he thought of home
And grit his teeth. He knew no help could come....

The silent sun over the earth held sway,
Occasional rifles cracked and far away
A heedless speck, a 'plane, slid on alone,
Like a fly traversing a cliff of stone.

"I must get back," said Gates aloud, and heaved
At his body. But it lay bereaved
Of any power. He could not wait till night....
And he lay still. Blood swam across his sight.
Then with a groan:
"No luck ever! Well, I must die alone."

Occasional rifles cracked. A cloud that shone,
Gold-rimmed, blackened the sun and then was gone....
The sun still smiled. The grass sang in its play.
Someone whistled: "Over the hills and far away."
Gates watched silently the swift, swift sun
Burning his life before it was begun....

Suddenly he heard Corporal Timmins' voice:

"Now then,
'Urry up with that tea."
"Hi Ginger!" "Bill!" His men!
Timmins and Jones and Wilkinson (the 'bard'),
And Hughes and Simpson. It was hard
Not to see them: Wilkinson, stubby, grim,
With his "No, sir," "Yes, sir," and the slim
Simpson: "Indeed, sir?" (while it seemed he winked
Because his smiling left eye always blinked)
And Corporal Timmins, straight and blonde and wise,
With his quiet-scanning, level, hazel eyes;
And all the others ... tunics that didn't fit....
A dozen different sorts of eyes. O it
Was hard to lie there! Yet he must. But no:
"I've got to die. I'll get to them. I'll go."

Inch by inch he fought, breathless and mute,
Dragging his carcase like a famished brute....
His head was hammering, and his eyes were dim;
A bloody sweat seemed to ooze out of him
And freeze along his spine.... Then he'd lie still
Before another effort of his will
Took him one nearer yard.

The parapet was reached.
He could not rise to it. A lookout screeched:
"Mr. Gates!"
Three figures in one breath
Leaped up. Two figures fell in toppling death;
And Gates was lifted in. "Who's hit?" said he.
"Timmins and Jones." "Why did they that for me?
I'm gone already!" Gently they laid him prone
And silently watched.
He twitched. They heard him moan
"Why for me?" His eyes roamed round, and none replied.
"I see it was alone I should have died."
They shook their heads. Then, "Is the doctor here?"
"He's coming, sir; he's hurryin', no fear."
"No good....
Lift me." They lifted him.
He smiled and held his arms out to the dim,
And in a moment passed beyond their ken,
Hearing him whisper, "O my men, my men!"

IN HOSPITAL, LONDON,
Autumn, 1915.

IV. BEHIND THE LINES: NIGHT, FRANCE

At the cross-roads I halt

And stand stock-still....
The linked and flickering constellations climb
Slowly the spread black heaven's immensity.

The wind wanders like a thought at fault.

Within the close-shuttered cottage nigh
I hear while its fearful, ag'd master sleeps like the dead
A slow clock chime
With solemn thrill
The most sombre hour of time,
And see stand in the cottage's garden chill
The two white crosses, one at each grave's head....

O France, France, France! I loved you, love you still;
But, Oh! why took you not my life instead?

V. AT THE WARS
Now that I am ta'en away,
And may not see another day,
What is it to my eye appears?
What sound rings in my stricken ears?
Not even the voice of any friend
Or eyes beloved-world-without-end,
But scenes and sounds of the countryside
In far England across the tide:
An upland field when Spring's begun,
Mellow beneath the evening sun....
A circle of loose and lichened wall
Over which seven red pines fall....
An orchard of wizen blossoming trees
Wherein the nesting chaffinches
Begin again the self-same song
All the late April day-time long....
Paths that lead a shelving course
Between the chalk scarp and the gorse
By English downs; and, O! too well
I hear the hidden, clanking bell
Of wandering sheep.... I see the brown
Twilight of the huge empty down....
Soon blotted out! for now a lane
Glitters with warmth of May-time rain,
And on a shooting briar I see
A yellow bird who sings to me.

O yellow-hammer, once I heard
Thy yaffle when no other bird
Could to my sunk heart comfort bring;
But now I would not have thee sing,
So sharp thy note is with the pain

Of England I may not see again!
Yet sing thy song: there answereth
Deep in me a voice which saith:
"The gorse upon the twilit down,
The English loam so sunset brown,
The bowed pines and the sheep-bells' clamour,
The wet, lit lane and the yellow-hammer,
The orchard and the chaffinch song,
Only to the Brave belong.
And he shall lose their joy for aye
If their price he cannot pay,
Who shall find them dearer far
Enriched by blood after long War."

VI. OUT OF TRENCHES: THE BARN, TWILIGHT

In the raftered barn we lie,
Sprawl, scrawl postcards, laugh and speak
Just mere men a trifle weary,
Worn in heart, a trifle weak:
Because alway
At close of day
Thought steals to England far away....
"Alf!" "O ay."
"Gi' us a tune, mate." "Well, wot say?"
"Swipe 'The Policeman's 'Oliday'...."
"Tiddle-iddle-um-tum,
Tum-TUM."

Sprawling on my aching back,
Think I nought; but I am glad
Dear, rare lads of pick and pack!
Aie me too! I'm sad.... I'm sad:
Some must die
(Maybe I):
O pray it take them suddenly!
"Bill!" "Wot ho!"
"Concertina: let it go
'If you were the Only Girl.'" "Cheero!"
"If you were the Only Girl."

Damn. 'Abide with Me....' Not now!
Well ... if you must: just your way.
It racks me till the tears nigh flow.
The tune see-saws. I turn, I pray
Behind my hand,
Shaken, unmanned,
In groans that God may understand:
Miracle!
"Let, let them all survive this hell."
Hear 'Trumpeter, what are you sounding?' swell.

(My God! I guess indeed too well:
The broken heart, eyes front, proud knell!)
Grant but mine sound with their farewell.
"It's the Last Post I'm sounding."

VII. BATTERY MOVING UP TO A NEW POSITION FROM REST CAMP: DAWN

Not a sign of life we rouse
In any square close-shuttered house
That flanks the road we amble down
Toward far trenches through the town.

The dark, snow-slushy, empty street....
Tingle of frost in brow and feet....
Horse-breath goes dimly up like smoke.
No sound but the smacking stroke

Of a sergeant flings each arm
Out and across to keep him warm,
And the sudden splashing crack
Of ice-pools broken by our track.

More dark houses, yet no sign
Of life.... An axle's creak and whine....
The splash of hooves, the strain of trace....
Clatter: we cross the market place.

Deep quiet again, and on we lurch
Under the shadow of a church:
Its tower ascends, fog-wreathed and grim;
Within its aisles a light burns dim....

When, marvellous! from overhead,
Like abrupt speech of one deemed dead,
Speech-moved by some Superior Will,
A bell tolls thrice and then is still.

And suddenly I know that now
The priest within, with shining brow,
Lifts high the small round of the Host.
The server's tingling bell is lost

In clash of the greater overhead.
Peace like a wave descends, is spread,
While watch the peasants' reverent eyes....

The bell's boom trembles, hangs, and dies.

O people who bow down to see
The Miracle of Calvary,
The bitter and the glorious,

Bow down, bow down and pray for us.

Once more our anguished way we take
Toward our Golgotha, to make
For all our lovers sacrifice.
Again the troubled bell tolls thrice.

And slowly, slowly, lifted up
Dazzles the overflowing cup.

O worshipping, fond multitude,
Remember us too, and our blood.

Turn hearts to us as we go by,
Salute those about to die,
Plead for them, the deep bell toll:
Their sacrifice must soon be whole.

Entreat you for such hearts as break
With the premonitory ache
Of bodies, whose feet, hands, and side,
Must soon be torn, pierced, crucified.

Sue for them and all of us
Who the world over suffer thus,
Who have scarce time for prayer indeed,
Who only march and die and bleed.

The town is left, the road leads on,
Bluely glaring in the sun,
Toward where in the sunrise gate
Death, honour, and fierce battle wait.

VIII. EVE OF ASSAULT: INFANTRY GOING DOWN TO TRENCHES
Downward slopes the wild red sun.
We lie around a waiting gun;
Soon we shall load and fire and load.
But, hark! a sound beats down the road.

"'Ello! wot's up?" "Let's 'ave a look!"
"Come on, Ginger, drop that book!"
"Wot an 'ell of bloody noise!"
"It's the Yorks and Lancs, meboys!"

So we crowd: hear, watch them come
One man drubbing on a drum,
A crazy, high mouth-organ blowing,
Tin cans rattling, cat-calls, crowing....

And above their rhythmic feet

A whirl of shrilling loud and sweet,
Round mouths whistling in unison;
Shouts: "'O's goin' to out the 'Un?

"Back us up, mates!" "Gawd, we will!"
"'Eave them shells at Kaiser Bill!"
"Art from Lancashire, melad?"
"Gi' 'en a cheer, boys; make 'en glad."

"'Ip 'urrah!" "Give Fritz the chuck."
"Good ol' bloody Yorks!" "Good-luck!"
"Cheer!"
I cannot cheer or speak
Lest my voice, my heart must break.

IX. THE ASSAULT

NOTE. (1) "Zero" is the hour agreed upon by the Staff when the infantry are to go over the parapet
and advance to the assault. (2) Guns are said to "lift" when, after pounding the front line of the
enemy, they lengthen their range and set up a barrier of fire behind his front line to prevent
supports moving up. Our infantry then advance.

The beating of the guns grows louder.
"Not long, boys, now."
My heart burns whiter, fearfuller, prouder.
Hurricanes grow
As guns redouble their fire.
Through the shaken periscope peeping,
I glimpse their wire:
Black earth, fountains of earth rise, leaping,
Spouting like shocks of meeting waves.
Death's fountains are playing.
Shells like shrieking birds rush over;
Crash and din rises higher.
A stream of lead raves
Over us from the left ... (we safe under cover!)
Crash! Reverberation! Crash!
Acrid smoke billowing. Flash upon flash.
Black smoke drifting. The German line
Vanishes in confusion, smoke. Cries, and cry
Of our men, "Gah, yer swine!
Ye're for it" die
In a hurricane of shell.

One cry:
"We're comin' soon! look out!"
There is opened hell
Over there; fragments fly,
Rifles and bits of men whirled at the sky:
Dust, smoke, thunder! A sudden bout
Of machine guns chattering....

And redoubled battering,
As if in fury at their daring!...

No good staring.

Time soon now ... home ... house on a sunny hill....
Gone like a flickered page:
Time soon now ... zero ... will engage....

A sudden thrill
"Fix bayonets!"
Gods! we have our fill
Of fear, hysteria, exultation, rage,
Rage to kill.

My heart burns hot, whiter and whiter,
Contracts tighter and tighter,
Until I stifle with the will
Long forged, now used
(Though utterly strained)
O pounding heart,
Baffled, confused,
Heart panged, head singing, dizzily pained
To do my part.

Blindness a moment. Sick.
There the men are!
Bayonets ready: click!
Time goes quick;
A stumbled prayer ... somehow a blazing star
In a blue night ... where?
Again prayer.
The tongue trips. Start:
How's time? Soon now. Two minutes or less.
The gun's fury mounting higher....
Their utmost. I lift a silent hand. Unseen I bless
Those hearts will follow me.
And beautifully,
Now beautifully my will grips.
Soul calm and round and filmed and white!

A shout: "Men, no such order as retire"
I nod.
The whistle's 'twixt my lips....
I catch
A wan, worn smile at me.
Dear men!
The pale wrist-watch....
The quiet hand ticks on amid the din.
The guns again
Rise to a last fury, to a rage, a lust:

Kill! Pound! Kill! Pound! Pound!
Now comes the thrust!
My part ... dizziness ... will ... but trust
These men. The great guns rise;
Their fury seems to burst the earth and skies!

They lift.

Gather, heart, all thoughts that drift;
Be steel, soul,
Compress thyself
Into a round, bright whole.
I cannot speak.

Time. Time!

I hear my whistle shriek,
Between teeth set;
I fling an arm up,
Scramble up the grime
Over the parapet!
I'm up. Go on.
Something meets us.
Head down into the storm that greets us.
A wail.
Lights. Blurr.
Gone.
On, on. Le[]a]d. Le[]a]d. Hail.
Spatter. Whirr! Whirr!
"Toward that patch of brown;
Direction left." Bullets a stream.
Devouring thought crying in a dream.
Men, crumpled, going down....
Go on. Go.
Deafness. Numbness. The loudening tornado.
Bullets. Mud. Stumbling and skating.
My voice's strangled shout:
"Steady pace, boys!"
The still light: gladness.
"Look, sir. Look out!"
Ha! ha! Bunched figures waiting.
Revolver levelled quick!
Flick! Flick!
Red as blood.
Germans. Germans.
Good! O good!
Cool madness.

X. THE LAST MORNING
Come now, O Death,

While I am proud,
While joy and awe are breath,
And heart beats loud!

While all around me stand
Men that I love,
The wind blares aloud, the grand
Sun wheels above.

Naked I stand to-day
Before my doom,
Welcome what comes my way,
Whatever come.

What is there more to ask
Than that I have?
Companions, love, a task,
And a deep grave!

Come then, Eternity,
If thou my lot;
Having been thus, I cannot be
As if I had not.

Naked I wait my doom!
Earth enough shroud!
Death, in thy narrow room
Man can lie proud!

XI. FULFILMENT

Was there love once? I have forgotten her.
Was there grief once? grief yet is mine.
Other loves I have, men rough, but men who stir
More grief, more joy, than love of thee and thine.

Faces cheerful, full of whimsical mirth,
Lined by the wind, burned by the sun;
Bodies enraptured by the abounding earth,
As whose children we are brethren: one.

And any moment may descend hot death
To shatter limbs! pulp, tear, blast
Beloved soldiers who love rough life and breath
Not less for dying faithful to the last.

O the fading eyes, the grimed face turned bony,
Oped mouth gushing, fallen head,
Lessening pressure of a hand shrunk, clammed, and stony!
O sudden spasm, release of the dead!

Was there love once? I have forgotten her.
Was there grief once? grief yet is mine.
O loved, living, dying, heroic soldier,
All, all, my joy, my grief, my love, are thine!

THE DEAD

I. THE BURIAL IN FLANDERS
(H. S. G., YPRES, 1916)

Through the light rain I think I see them going,
Through the light rain under the muffled skies;
Across the fields a stealthy wet wind wanders,
The mist bedews their tunics, dizzies their brains.

Shoulder-high, khaki shoulder by shoulder,
They bear my Boy upon his last journey.
Night is closing. The wind sighs, ebbs, and falters....
They totter dreaming, deem they see his face.

Even as Vikings of old their slaughtered leader
Upon their shoulders, so now bear they on
All that remains of Boy, my friend, their leader,
An officer who died for them under the dawn.

O that I were there that I might carry,
Might share that bitter load in grief, in pride!...
I see upon bronze faces love, submission,
And a dumb sorrow for that cheerful Boy.

Now they arrive. The priest repeats the service.
The drifting rain obscures.
They are dispersed.
The dying sun streams out: a moment's radiance;
The still, wet, glistening grave; the trod sward steaming.

Sudden great guns startle, echoing on the silence.
Thunder. Thunder.
HE HAS FALLEN IN BATTLE.
(O Boy! Boy!)
Lessening now. The rain
Patters anew. Far guns rumble and shudder
And night descends upon the desolate plain.

LAWFORD,
September, 1916.

II. BOY
In a far field, away from England, lies

A Boy I friended with a care like love;
All day the wide earth aches, the cold wind cries,
The melancholy clouds drive on above.

There, separate from him by a little span,
Two eagle cousins, generous, reckless, free,
Two Grenfells, lie, and my Boy is made man,
One with these elder knights of chivalry.

Boy, who expected not this dreadful day,
Yet leaped, a soldier, at the sudden call,
Drank as your fathers, deeper though than they,
The soldier's cup of anguish, blood, and gall,

Not now as friend, but as a soldier, I
Salute you fallen; for the Soldier's name
Our greatest honour is, if worthily
These wayward hearts assume and bear the same:

The Soldier's is a name none recognize,
Saving his fellows. Deeds are all his flower.
He lives, he toils, he suffers, and he dies,
And if not all in vain this is his dower:

The Soldier is the Martyr of a nation,
Expresses but is subject to its will;
His is the Pride ennobles Resignation,
As his the rebel Spirit-to-fulfil.

Anonymous, he takes his country's name,
Becomes its blindest vassal though its lord
By force of arms; its shame is called his shame,
As its the glory gathered by his sword.

Lonely he is: he has nor friend nor lover,
Sith in his body he is dedicate....
His comrades only share his life, or offer
Their further deeds to one more heart oblate.

Living, he's made an 'Argument Beyond'
For others' peace; but when hot wars have birth,
For all his brothers' safety becomes bond
To Fate or Whatsoever sways this Earth.

Dying, his mangled body, to inter it,
He doth bequeath him into comrade hands;
His soul he renders to some Captain Spirit
That knows, admires, pities, and understands!

All this you knew by that which doth reside
Deeper than learning; by apprehension

Of ancient, dark, and melancholy pride
You were a Soldier true, and died as one.

All day the cold wind cries, the clouds unroll;
But to the cloud and wind I cry, "Be still!"
What need of comfort has the heroic soul?
What soldier finds a soldier's grave is chill?

LAWFORD,
September, 1916.

III. PLAINT OF FRIENDSHIP BY DEATH BROKEN
(R. P., LOOS, 1915)

God, if Thou livest, Thine eye on me bend,
And stay my grief and bring my pain to end:
Pain for my lost, the deepest, rarest friend
Man ever had, whence groweth this despair.

I had a friend: but, O! he is now dead;
I had a vision: for which he has bled:
I had happiness: but it is fled.
God help me now, for I must needs despair.

His eyes were dark and sad, yet never sad;
In them moved sombre figures sable-clad;
They were the deepest eyes man ever had,
They were my solemn joy, now my despair.

In my perpetual night they on me look,
Reading me slowly; and I cannot brook
Their silent beauty, for nor crack nor nook
Can cover me but they shall find me there.

His face was straight, his mouth was wide yet trim;
His hair was tangled black, and through its dim
Softness his perplexed hand would writhe and swim
Hands that were small on arms strong-knit yet spare.

He stood no taller than our common span,
Swam but nor farther leaped nor faster ran;
I know him spirit now, who seemed a man.
God help me now, for I must needs despair.

His voice was low and clear, yet it could rise
And beat in indignation at the skies;
Then no man dared to meet his fire-filled eyes,
And even I, his own friend, did not dare.

With humorous wistfulness he spoke to us,

Yet there was something more mysterious,
Beyond his words or silence, glorious:
I know not what, but we could feel it there.

I mind now how we sat one winter night
While past his open window raced the bright
Snow-torrent golden in the hot firelight....
I see him smiling at the streamered air.

I watched him to the open window go,
And lean long smiling, whispering to the snow,
Play with his hands amid the fiery flow
And when he turned it flamed amid his hair.

Without arose a sudden bell's huge clang
Until a thousand bells in answer rang
And midnight Oxford hummed and reeled and sang
Under the whitening fury of the air.

His figure standing in the fiery room....
Behind him the snow seething through the gloom....
The great bells shaking, thundering out their doom....
Soft Fiery Snow and Night his being were.

Yet he could be simply glad and take his choice,
Walking spring woods, mimicking each bird voice;
When he was glad we learned how to rejoice:
If the birds sing, 'tis to my spite they dare.

All women loved him, yet his mother won
His tenderness alone, for Moon and Sun
And Rain were for him sister, brother, lovèd one,
And in their life he took an equal share.

Strength he had, too; strength of unrusted will
Buttressed his natural charity, and ill
Fared it with him who sought his good to kill:
He was its Prince and Champion anywhere.

Yet he had weakness, for he burned too fast;
And his unrecked-of body at the last
He in impatience on the bayonets cast,
Body whose spirit had outsoared them there.

I had a friend, but, O! he is now dead.
Fate would not let me follow where he led.
In him I had happiness. But he is dead.
God help me now, for I must needs despair.

God, if Thou livest, and indeed didst send
Thine only Son to be to all a Friend,

Bid His dark, pitying eyes upon me bend,
And His hand heal, or I must needs despair.

IN HOSPITAL,
Autumn, 1915.

IV. BY THE WOOD

How still the day is, and the air how bright!
A thrush sings and is silent in the wood;
The hillside sleeps dizzy with heat and light;
A rhythmic murmur fills the quietude;
A woodpecker prolongs his leisured flight,
Rising and falling on the solitude.

But there are those who far from yon wood lie,
Buried within the trench where all were found.
A weight of mould oppresses every eye,
Within that cabin close their limbs are bound,
And there they rot amid the long profound,
Disastrous silence of grey earth and sky.

These once, too, rested where now rests but one,
Who scarce can lift his panged and heavy head,
Who drinks in grief the hot light of the sun,
Whose eyes watch dully the green branches spread,
Who feels his currents ever slowlier run,
Whose lips repeat a silent '... Dead! all dead!'

O youths to come shall drink air warm and bright,
Shall hear the bird cry in the sunny wood,
All my Young England fell to-day in fight:
That bird, that wood, was ransomed by our blood!

I pray you when the drum rolls let your mood
Be worthy of our deaths and your delight.

1916.

THE AFTERMATH

I. AT THE EBB

Alone upon the monotonous ocean's verge
I take my stand, and view with heavy eye
The grey wave rise. I hear its sullen surge,
Its bubbling rush and sudden downward sigh....

My friends are dead ... there fades from me the light
Of her warm face I loved; upon me stare
In the dull noon or deadest hour of night

The smiling lips and chill eyes of Despair.

A light wind blows.... I hear the low wave steal
In and collapse like a despondent breath.
My life has ebbed: I neither see nor feel:
I am suspended between life and death.

Again the wave caves in. O, I am worn
Smoother than any pebble on the beach!
I would dissolve to that whence I was born,
Or alway bide beyond the long wave's reach.

O Will, thou only strengthener of man's heart
When all is gone, love and the love of friends,
When even Earth's comfort has become a part
Of that futility nor breaks nor mends:

Strengthen me now against these utmost wrongs;
Stay my wrecked spirit within thy control,
That men may find some fury in my songs
Which, like strong wine, shall fortify the soul.

BENEATH GOLD CAP,
June, 1916.

II. ALONE

The grey wind and the grey sea
Tossing under the long grey sky....
My heart is lonelier than the wind;
My heart is emptier than the sky,
And beats more heavily
Than the cold surge beneath the gull,
Wheeling with his reiterant cry
Of loneliness.... All, all is lone:
Alone!...
And so am I.

III. THANKSGIVING

Amazement fills my heart to-night,
Amaze and awful fears;
I am a ship that sees no light,
But blindly onward steers.

Flung toward heaven's toppling rage,
Sunk between steep and steep,
A lost and wondrous fight I wage
With the embattled deep.

I neither know nor care at length

Where drives the storm about;
Only I summon all my strength
And swear to ride it out.

Yet give I thanks; despite these wars,
My ship, though blindly blown,
Long lost to sun or moon or stars
Still stands up alone.
I need no trust in borrowed spars;
My strength is yet my own.

IV. ANNIHILATED
Upon the sweltering sea's enormous round,
Asmoke, adazzle, brown and brown and gold,
A hushed light falls....
Then clouds without a sound
Darken the sea within their curtain's fold.

The sombre clouds through which the sick sun climbs
Smoke slowly on. Below there is no breath.
The long black beach turns livid.
The sea chimes.
I taste the fulness of my spirit's death.

V. SHUT OF NIGHT
The sea darkens. Waves roar and rush.
The wind rises. The last birds haste.
One star over eve's bitter flush
Spills on the spouting waste.

Loud and louder the darkened sea.
The wind shrills on a monotone.
Sky and deep, wrecked confusedly,
Travail and cry as one.

Long I look on the deepening sky,
The chill star, the forlorn sea breaking;
For what does my spirit cry?
For what is my heart so aching?

Is it home? but I have no home.
Is it tears? but I no more weep.
Is it love? love went by dumb.
Is it sleep? but I would not sleep.

Must I fare, then, in fear and fever
On a journey become thrice far
Whose sun has gone down for ever,
Whose night brings no guiding star?

The wind roars, and an ashen beam
Waving up shrinks away in haste.
The waves crash. The star's trickling gleam
Travels the warring waste.

I look up. In the windy height
The lone orb, serene and afar,
Shakes with excess of her light....

Beauty, be thou my star!

VI. THE FULL HEART

Alone on the shore in the pause of the night-time
I stand and I hear the long wind blow light;
I view the constellations quietly, quietly burning;
I hear the wave fall in the hush of the night.

Long after I am dead, ended this bitter journey,
Many another whose heart holds no light
Shall your solemn sweetness, hush, awe, and comfort,
O my companions, Wind, Waters, Stars, and Night.

NEAR GOLD CAP,
1916.

VII. SONNET: OUR DEAD

They have not gone from us. O no! they are
The inmost essence of each thing that is
Perfect for us; they flame in every star;
The trees are emerald with their presences.
They are not gone from us; they do not roam
The flaw and turmoil of the lower deep,
But have now made the whole wide world their home,
And in its loveliness themselves they steep.

They fail not ever; theirs is the diurn
Splendour of sunny hill and forest grave;
In every rainbow's glittering drop they burn;
They dazzle in the massed clouds' architrave;
They chant on every wind, and they return
In the long roll of any deep blue wave.

VIII. DELIVERANCE

Out of the Night! out of the Night I come:
Free at last: the whole world is my home:
I have lost self: I look not on myself again,
But if I do I see a man among men.

Out of the Night! out of the Night, O Flesh:
Soul I know not from Body within thy mesh:
Accepting all that is, I cannot divide the same:
I accept the smoke because I accept the flame.

Out of the Night! out of the Night, O Friends:
O all my dead, think ye our friendship ends?
Harold, Kenneth, Dick, many hearts that were true,
While I breathe breath, I am breathing you.

Out of the Night! out of the Night, O Power:
Many a fight to be won, many an awful hour;
Many an hour to wish death ere I go to death,
Many an hour to bless breath ere I cease from breath.

Out of the Night! out of the Night, O Soul:
Give thanks to the Night: Night and Day are the Whole.
I count mere life-breath nothing now I know Life's worth
Lies all in spending! that known, love Life and Earth.

Address To The Sunset
Exquisite stillness! What serenities
Of earth and air! How bright atop the wall
The stonecrop's fire and beyond the precipice
How huge, how hushed the primrose evenfall!
How softly, too, the white crane voyages
Yon honeyed height of warmth and silence,
whence
He can look down on islet, lake and shore
And crowding woods and voiceless promontories
Or, further gazing, view the magnificence
Of cloud- like mountains and of mountainous cloud
Or ghostly wrack below the horizon rim
Not even his eye has vantage to explore.
Now, spirit, find out wings and mount to him,
Wheel where he wheels, where he is soaring soar.
Hang where now he hangs in the planisphere
Evening's first star and golden as a bee
In the sun's hair - for happiness is here!

Evenstar
Evenstar, still evenstar
If this twilight thou dost shine
On a more unhappy head,

On tears lonelier than mine,
Vainer prayers and deepest sighs,
Take, sweet spirit, thou that art
Comforter of our despairs
All the prayers perforce unsaid,
All the sighs I cannot sigh,
All the tears I cannot shed;
Fill his eyes and flood his heart,
Who, my everlasting kin,
Broods, afar, unknown, apart.
Bring, ah bring him that surcease
From unsolaceable pain,
Which nor prayers, nor tears, nor sighs,
No, nor even the divine
Presence of thy eternal peace
Can, O evenstar, make mine.

Farewell

For the last time, maybe, upon the knoll
I stand. The eve is golden, languid, sad.
Day like a tragic actor plays his role
To the last whispered word and falls gold-clad.
I, too, take leave of all I ever had.

They shall not say I went with heavy heart:
Heavy I am, but soon I shall be free,
I love them all, but oh I now depart
A little sadly, strangely, fearfully,
As one who goes to try a mystery.

The bell is sounding down in Dedham vale:
Be still, O bell: too often standing here
When all the air was tremulous, fine and pale,
Thy golden note so calm, so still, so clear,
Out of my stony heart has struck a tear.

And now tears are not mine. I have release
From all the former and the later pain,
Like the mid sea I rock in boundless peace
Soothed by the charity of the deep-sea rain….
Calm rain! Calm sea! Calm found, long sought in vain!

O bronzen pines, evening of gold and blue,
Steep mellow slope, brimmed twilit pools below,
Hushed trees, still vale dissolving in the dew,
Farewell. Farewell. There is no more to do.
We have been happy. Happy now I go.

Fulfilment

Was there love once? I have forgotten her.
Was there grief once? Grief yet is mine.
Other loves I have, men rough, but men who stir
More grief, more joy, than love of thee and thine.

Faces cheerful, full of whimsical mirth,
Lined by the wind, burned by the sun;
Bodies enraptured by the abounding earth,
As whose children we are brethern: one.

And any moment may descend hot death
To shatter limbs! Pulp, tear, blast
Belovèd soldiers who love rough life and breath
Not less for dying faithful to the last.

O the fading eyes, the grimed face turned bony,
Oped mouth gushing, fallen head,
Lessening pressure of a hand, shrunk, clammed and stony!
O sudden spasm, release of the dead!

Was there love once? I have forgotten her.
Was there grief once? Grief yet is mine.
O loved, living, dying, heroic soldier,
All, all my joy, my grief, my love, are thine.

I Must Remember Now
I must remember now how once I woke
To find the harsh lamplight stream upon her bed,
The ceiling tremble in its giddy smoke,
And on the wall the agile spider spread,
To hear the reverberate vault of silence shake
Beneath the hollow crash of midnight's toil,
Whose profound strokes waned impotent to break
The charnel stillness of the city's soul.
These I remember, but would more forget
What is most fixed, whereby I am undone,
How white, how still you lay, though shuddering yet
In the last luxury of oblivion,
As if of Death you had taken love long denied,
With on your face the bliss of suicide.

Nearer
Nearer and ever nearer...
My body, tired but tense,
Hovers 'twixt vague pleasure
And tremulous confidence.

Arms to have and to use them
And a soul to be made

Worthy, if not worthy;
If afraid, unafraid.

To endure for a little,
To endure and have done:
Men I love about me,
Over me the sun!

And should at last suddenly
Fly the speeding death,
The four great quarters of heaven
Receive this littlle breath.

Night Rhapsody
How beautiful it is to wake at night,
When over all there reigns the ultimate spell
Of complete silence, darkness absolute,
To feel the world, tilted on axle-tree,
In slow gyration, with no sensible sound,
Unless to ears of unimagined beings,
Resident incorporeal or stretched
In vigilance of ecstasy among
Ethereal paths and the celestial maze.
The rumour of our onward course now brings
A steady rustle, as of some strange ship
Darkling with soundless sail all set and amply filled
By volume of an ever-constant air,
At fullest night, through seas for ever calm,
Swept lovely and unknown for ever on.

How beautiful it is to wake at night,
Embalmed in darkness watchful, sweet, and still,
As is the brain's mood flattered by the swim
Of currents circumvolvent in the void,
To lie quite still and to become aware
Of the dim light cast by nocturnal skies
On a dim earth beyond the window-ledge,
So, isolate from the friendly company
Of the huge universe which turns without,
To brood apart in calm and joy awhile
Until the spirit sinks and scarcely knows
Whether self is, or if self only is,
For ever....

How beautiful to wake at night,
Within the room grown strange, and still, and sweet,
And live a century while in the dark
The dripping wheel of silence slowly turns;
To watch the window open on the night,
A dewy silent deep where nothing stirs,

And, lying thus, to feel dilate within
The press, the conflict, and the heavy pulse
Of incommunicable sad ecstasy,
Growing until the body seems outstretched
In perfect crucifixion on the arms
Of a cross pointing from last void to void,
While the heart dies to a mere midway spark.

All happiness thou holdest, happy night,
For such as lie awake and feel dissolved
The peaceful spice of darkness and the cool
Breath hither blown from the ethereal flowers
That mist thy fields! O happy, happy wounds,
Conditioned by existence in humanity,
That have such powers to heal them! slow sweet sighs
Torn from the bosom, silent wails, the birth
Of such long-treasured tears as pain his eyes,
Who, waking, hears the divine solicitudes
Of midnight with ineffable purport charged.

How beautiful it is to wake at night,
Another night, in darkness yet more still,
Save when the myriad leaves on full-fledged boughs,
Filled rather by the perfume's wandering flood
Than by dispansion of the still sweet air,
Shall from the furthest utter silences
In glimmering secrecy have gathered up
An host of whisperings and scattered sighs,
To loose at last a sound as of the plunge
And lapsing seethe of some Pacific wave,
Which, risen from the star-thronged outer troughs,
Rolls in to wreathe with circling foam away
The flutter of the golden moths that haunt
The star's one glimmer daggered on wet sands.

So beautiful it is to wake at night!
Imagination, loudening with the surf
Of the midsummer wind among the boughs,
Gathers my spirit from the haunts remote
Of faintest silence and the shades of sleep,
To bear me on the summit of her wave
Beyond known shores, beyond the mortal edge
Of thought terrestrial, to hold me poised
Above the frontiers of infinity,
To which in the full reflux of the wave
Come soon I must, bubble of solving foam,
Borne to those other shores — now never mine
Save for a hovering instant, short as this
Which now sustains me ere I be drawn back
To learn again, and wholly learn, I trust,
How beautiful it is to wake at night.

November

As I walk the misty hill
All is languid, fogged, and still;
Not a note of any bird
Nor any motion's hint is heard,
Save from soaking thickets round
Trickle or water's rushing sound,
And from ghostly trees the drip
Of runnel dews or whispering slip
Of leaves, which in a body launch
Listlessly from the stagnant branch
To strew the marl, already strown,
With litter sodden as its own,

A rheum, like blight, hangs on the briars,
And from the clammy ground suspires
A sweet frail sick autumnal scent
Of stale frost furring weeds long spent;
And wafted on, like one who sleeps,
A feeble vapour hangs or creeps,
Exhaling on the fungus mould
A breath of age, fatigue, and cold.

Oozed from the bracken's desolate track,
By dark rains havocked and drenched black.
A fog about the coppice drifts,
Or slowly thickens up and lifts
Into the moist, despondent air.

Mist, grief, and stillness everywhere....

And in me, too, there is no sound
Save welling as of tears profound,
Where in me cloud, grief, stillness reign,
And an intolerable pain
Begins.
Rolled on as in a flood there come
Memories of childhood, boyhood, home,
And that which, sudden, pangs me most,
Thought of the first-belov'd, long lost,
Too easy lost! My cold lips frame
Tremulously the familiar name,
Unheard of her upon my breath:
'Elizabeth. Elizabeth.'

No voice answers on the hill,
All is shrouded, sad, and still ...
Stillness, fogged brakes, and fog on high.
Only in me the waters cry

Who mourn the hours now slipped forever,
Hours of boding, joy, and fever,
When we loved, by chance beguiled,
I a boy and you a child —
Child! but with an angel's air,
Astonished, eager, unaware,
Or elfin's, wandering with a grace
Foreign to any fireside race,
And with a gaiety unknown
In the light feet and hair backblown,
And with a sadness yet more strange,
In meagre cheeks which knew to change
Or faint or fired more swift than sight,
And forlorn hands and lips pressed white,
And fragile voice, and head downcast,
Hiding tears, lifted at the last
To speed with one pale smile the wise
Glance of the grey immortal eyes.

How strange it was that we should dare
Compound a miracle so rare
As, 'twixt this pace and Time's next pace,
Each to discern th' elected's face!
Yet stranger that the high sweet fire,
In hearts nigh foreign to desire,
Could burn, sigh, weep, and burn again
As oh, it never has since then!
Most strange of all that we so young
Dared learn but would not speak love's tongue,
Love pledged but in the reveries
Of our sad and dreaming eyes....

Now upon such journey bound me,
Grief, disquiet, and stillness round me,
As bids me where I cannot tell,
Turn I and sigh, unseen, farewell.
Breathe the name as soft as mist,
Lips, which nor kissed her nor were kissed!
And again — a sigh, a death
'Elizabeth. Elizabeth.'

No voice answers; but the mist
Glows for a moment amethyst
Ere the hid sun dissolves away,
And dimness, growing dimmer grey,
Hides all ... till nothing can I see
But the blind walls enclosing me,
And no sound and no motion hear
But the vague water throbbing near,
Sole voice upon the darkening hill
Where all is blank and dead and still.

O Nightingale My Heart

O Nightingale my heart
How sad thou art!
How heavy is thy wing,
Desperately whirrëd that thy throat may fling
Song to the tingling silences remote!
Thine eye whose ruddy spark
Burned fiery of late,
How dead and dark!
Why so soon didst thou sing,
And with such turbulence of love and hate?

Learn that there is no singing yet can bring
The expected dawn more near;
And thou art spent already, though the night
Scarce has begun;
What voice, what eyes wilt thou have for the light
When the light shall appear,
And O what wings to bear thee t'ward the Sun?

PÆan

Upon seeing a portrait of Blake

Something moves in his dust,
Flame sleeps beneath the crust;
O whence had he those eyes
Lit with celestial surprise?
From what world blew that gust?
Are we near to Paradise?

Gather a chaplet of five stars
And the opalescent hue
Of the aureole brightness cast
Red, hardly red, and blue, scarce blue,
Round th' immaculate frosty moon,
Splintering light in glacial spars,
When November's loudening blast
Sweeps heaven's floor till burnished
More crystal than at August noon,
So we fit radiance may cast
Before his feet, around his head.

How visits he an earthly place,
Wanders among a mortal race?
How were his footsteps led
That still about his face
Lingers a ghostly trace
Of a secret influence shed

By a Hand the world denies,
In a land her most son flies,
As a gift upon him thrust
For an end he knoweth not,
Yet will shine because he must,
Shine and sing because he must
Reap a wrong he soweth not
Of contempt anger and distrust
For a world which boweth not
To the Flame which binds our dust.

Go net the moon, go snare the sun,
Set them upon his either hand!
Beneath his heels Leviathan
Roll your thick coils! His head be spanned
By rainbows tripled! Set a gem
At the Cross-scabbard of his sword
Whiter than lambwool or lilystem!
Place on his brow the diadem
Given the warrior of the Lord,
The crown-turrets of Jerusalem!

Seventeen
All the loud winds were in the garden wood,
All shadows joyfuller than lissom hounds
Doubled in chasing, all exultant clouds
That ever flung fierce mist and eddying fire
Across heavens deeper than blue polar seas
Fled over the sceptre-spikes of the chestnuts,
Over the speckle of the wych-elms' green.
She shouted; then stood still, hushed and abashed
To hear her voice so shrill in that gay roar,
And suddenly her eyelashes were dimmed,
Caught in tense tears of spiritual joy;
For there were daffodils which sprightly shook
Ten thousand ruffling heads throughout the wood,
And every flower of those delighting flowers
Laughed, nodding to her, till she clapped her hands
Crying 'O daffies, could you only speak!'

But there was more. A jay with skyblue shaft
Set in blunt wing, skimmed screaming on ahead.
She followed him. A murrey squirrel eyed
Her warily, cocked upon tail-plumed haunch,
Then, skipping the whirligig of last-year leaves,
Whisked himself out of sight and reappeared
Leering about the hole of a young beech;
And every time she thought to corner him
He scrambled round on little scratchy hands
To peek at her about the other side.

She lost him, bolting branch to branch, at last
The impudent brat! But still high overhead
Flight on exuberant flight of opal scud,
Or of dissolving mist, florid as flame.

Scattered in ecstasy over the blue. And she
Followed, first walking, giving her bright locks
To the cold fervour of the springtime gale,
Whose rush bore the cloud shadow past the cloud
Over the irised wastes of emerald turf.
And still the huge wind volleyed. Save the gulls,
Goldenly in the sunny blast careering
Or on blue-shadowed underwing at plunge,
None shared with her who now could not but run
The splendour and tumult of th' onrushing spring.

And now she ran no more: the gale gave plumes.
One with the shadows whirled along the grass,
One with the onward smother of veering gulls,
One with the pursuit of cloud after cloud,
Swept she. Pure speed coursed in immortal limbs;
Nostrils drank as from wells of unknown air;
Ears received the smooth silence of racing floods;
Light as of glassy suns froze in her eyes;
Space was given her and she ruled all space.

Spring, author of twifold loveliness,
Who flittest in the mirth of the wild folk,
Profferest greeting in the faces of flowers,
Blowest in the firmamental glory,
Renewest in the heart of the sad human
All faiths, guard thou the innocent spirit
Into whose unknowing hands this noontide
Thou pourest treasure, yet scarce recognised,
That unashamed before man's glib wisdom,
Unabashed beneath the wrath of chance,
She accept in simplicity of homage
The hidden holiness, the created emblem
To be in her, until death shall take her,
The source and secret of eternal spring.

The Flower Of Flame

I

As round the cliff I came alone
The whole bay bared its blaze to me;
Loud sang the wind, the wild sun shone
The tumbled clouds fled scattering on,
Light shattered on wave and winking stone,

And in the glassy midst stood one
Brighter than sun or cloud or sea.

She with flame-vehement hair untied,
Virginal in her fluttering dress,
Watched, deafened and all dazzle-eyed,
Each opulent breaker's crash and glide
And now flung arms up high and wide
As if, possessing all, she cried
Her beauty, youth and happiness.

Loud rang the waves and higher, higher
The surge in chains of light was flung,
The wind as in a wild desire
Licked round her form—she seemed a spire
Of sunny drift ! a fount of fire!
The hymn of some triumphant lyre
Which sounded when the world was young!

Purified by the scalding glare,
Swept clear by the salty sea-wind's flow,
My eyes knew you for what you are
The daemon thing for which we dare,
Which breaks us, which we bid not spare.
The life, the light, the heavenly snare,
The turretted city's overthrow,
Helen, I knew you standing there!

II
The long, low wavelets of summer
Glide in and glitter along the sand;
The fitful breezes of summer
Blow fragrantly from the land.

Side by side we lie silent
Between sunned cliffs and blown seas:
Our eyes more bright than sea ripples,
Our breaths more light than the breeze.

When a gust meets a wave that advances
The wave leaps, flames, falls with a hiss
So lightly, so brightly each heart leaps
When our dumb lips touch in a kiss.

III
Foamless the gradual waters well
From the sheer deep, where darkness lies,
Till to the shoulder rock they swell
With a slow cumulance of sighs.

O, waters gather up your strength
From the blind caves of your unrest,
Loose your load utterly at length
Over the moonlight-marbled breast.

There sleep, diffused, the long dim hours,
Nor let your love-locks be withdrawn
Till round the world-horizon glowers
The wrath and chaos of the dawn.

IV
She picked a whorled shell from the beach
And laid it close beside her ear;
Then held it, frightened, at full reach
Toward my face that I might hear.

And while she leaned and while I heard
Our dumb eyes dared not meet for shame,
Our hearts within us sickly stirred,
Our limbs ran wax before the flame.

For in the despairing voice and meek
An echo to our hearts we found
Who through love-striving vainly seek
To coop the infinite in bound.

V
All is estranged to-day.
Chastened and meek,
Side by side taking our way,
With what anguish we seek
To dare each to face the other or even to speak!

The sun like an opal drifts
Through a vapourous shine
Or overwhelms itself in dark rifts,
On the sea's far line
Sheer light falls in a single sword like a sign.

The sea, striving in its bed
Like a corpse that awakes,
Slowly heaves up its lustreless head,
Crowned with weeds and snakes,
To strike at the shore bareing fangs as it breaks.

Something threatening earth
Aims at our love;
Gone is our ignorant mirth,

Love like speech of the dove;
The Sword and the Snake have seen and proclaim now
'Enough!'

VI
The narrow pathway winds its course
Through dwarfish oaks and junipers
Till suddenly beyond the gorse
We glimpse the copse of stunted firs,

That tops the headland, round whose base
The cold tide flings a drowned man's bones
All day against the cliff's sheer face,
All night prolongs his lasting groans.

The Drowned—who in the copse once stood
Waiting the Dead: to end both vows—
Heard, as we hear, the split of wood
And shrieking of the writhen boughs

Grow shrill and shriller. Pass the spot,
The strained boughs arch toward collapse.
A whistle and—CRACK! there's the shot!
Or is it but a bough which snaps?

Ever, when we have left the gorse
And through the copse each hastening hies,
We, lovers on the self-same course,
Dare not look in each other's eyes.

VII
Before I woke I knew her gone
Though nothing nigh had stirred,
Now by the curtain inward blown
She stood not seen but heard
Where the faint moonlight dimmed or shone . . .
And neither spoke a word.

One hand against her mouth she pressed,
But could not staunch its cry,
The other knocked upon her breast
Impotently . . . while I
Glared rigid, labouring, possessed
And dared not ask her why.

VIII
Noon : and now rocks the summer sea
All idleness, one gust alone

Skates afar off and soundlessly
Is gone from me as you are gone.

No hull creeps on th' horizon's rim
No pond of smoke wreathes the far sky,
Only the dazzling sinuous swim
Of the fierce tide-maze scalds the eye.

Alone, aloft, unendingly
A peering gull on moveless wing
Floats silent by and again by
In search for some indefinite thing.

Each wave-line glittering through its run
Gives, in its plash where still pools lie
Upstaring at the downstaring sun,
A single harsh and sudden sigh.

And Oh, more lonely blows the breeze,
More empty shines the perfect sky,
More solitary sound the seas
Where two watched, where now watch but I!

IX
I love a flower which has no lover
The yellow sea-poppy is its name;
Spined leaves its glaucous green stem cover
Its flower is a yellow fitful flame.

Stung by the spray which leaps the shingle,
Torn by the winds that scour the beach,
Its roots with the salt sea-wrack mingle
Its leaves upon the bleached stones bleach.

Its desperate growth but few remember,
None misses it when it has died
Scorched by the sun to a scant ember
Or wholly ravaged by the tide.

Yet I elect this weed to cherish
Nor any other would desire
Than this which must so shortly perish
Tortured by sea-foam or sky-fire.

Above this flower we too once bended,
Drawn to it by a subtle spell,
On whom the fire of heaven descended
Over whom the wave arose from hell.

Frantic, she snatched the ragged blossom,

Kissed it then with a wild, fierce kiss,
Pressed spine and flame into her bosom,
Crying, 'The flower! our love is this!'

The grey waves crash. The wind whirls over.
The flower is withered from the beach,
Whose waves divide the loved and lover,
Whose wind blows louder than their speech.

X
The moon behind high tranquil leaves
Hides her sad head;
The dwindled water tinkles and grieves
In the stream's black bed
And where now, where are you sleeping?
The shadowy nightjar, hawking gnats,
Flickers or floats;
High in still air the flurrying bats
Repeat their wee notes,
And where now, where are you sleeping?

Silent lightning flutters in heaven,
Where quiet crowd
By the toil of an upper whirlwind driven
Dark legions of cloud;
In whose arms now are you sleeping?
The cloud makes, lidding the sky's wan hole,
The world a tomb;
Far out at sea long thunders roll
From gloom to dim gloom;
In whose arms now are you sleeping?

Rent clouds, like boughs, in darkness hang
Close overhead;
The foreland's bell-buoy begins to clang
As if for the dead:
Awake they, where you are sleeping?
The chasms crack; the heavens revolt;
With tearing sound
Bright bolt volleys on flaring bolt,
Wave and cloud clash; through deep, through vault
Huge thunders rebound!
But they wake not where you are sleeping.

The Last Salute
In a far field, away from England, lies
A boy I friended with a care like love;
All day the wide earth aches, the keen wind cries,
The melancholy clouds drive on above.

There, separate from him by a little span
Two eagle cousins, generous, reckless, free,
Two Grenfells, lie, and my boy is made man,
One with these elder knights of chivalry.

Boy, who expected not this dreadful day,
Yet leaped, a soldier, at the sudden call,
Drank as your fathers, deeper though than they,
The soldier's cup of anguish, blood, and gall.

Not now as friend, but as a soldier, I
Salute you fallen. For the soldier's name
Our greatest honour is, if worthily
These wayward hearts assume and bear the same

The Soldier's is a name none recognise
Saving his fellows. Deeds are all his flower.
He lives, he toils, he suffers, and he dies,
And if not vainly spent, this is his dower.

The Soldier is the Martyr of a nation,
Expresses but is subject to its will,
His is the Pride ennobles Resignation
As his the rebel Spirit-to-fulfil.

Anonymous, he takes his country's name,
Becomes its blindest vassal - though its lord
By force of arms-its shame is called his shame,
As its the glory gathered by his sword.

Lonely he is: he has nor friend nor lover,
Sith in his body he is dedicate...
His comrades only share his life and offer
Their further deeds to one more heart oblate.

Living, lie's made an 'Argument Beyond'
For others' peace; but when hot wars have birth,
For all his brothers' safety he is bond
To Fate or Whatsoever sways this Earth.

Dying, his mangled body, to inter it,
He doth bequeath him into comrade hands,
His soul he renders to some Captain Spirit
That knows, admires, pities, and understands!

All this you knew by that which doth reside
Deeper than learning; by apprehension
Of ancient, dark, and melancholy pride;
You were a Soldier true and died as one!...

All day the long wind cries, the clouds unroll,
But to the cloud and wind I cry, 'Be still!'
What need of comfort has the heroic soul?
What soldier finds a soldier's grave is chill?

The Pilgrim

Put by the sun my joyful soul,
We are for darkness that is whole;

Put by the wine, now for long years
We must be thirsty with salt tears;

Put by the rose, bind thou instead
The fiercest thorns about thy head;

Put by the courteous tire, we need
But the poor pilgrim's blackest weed;

Put by — a'beit with tears — thy lute,
Sing but to God or else be mute.

Take leave of friends save such as dare
Thy love with Loneliness to share.

It is full tide. Put by regret.
Turn, turn away. Forget. Forget.

Put by the sun my lightless soul,
We are for darkness that is whole.

The Sprig of Lime

He lay, and those who watched him were amazed
To see unheralded beneath the lids
Twin tears, new-gathered at the price of pain,
Start and at once run crookedly athwart
Cheeks channelled long by pain, never by tears.
So desolate too the sigh next uttered
They had wept also, but his great lips moved,
And bending down one heard, 'A sprig of lime;
Bring me a sprig of lime.' Whereat she stole
With dumb signs forth to pluck the thing he craved.

So lay he till a lime-twig had been snapped
From some still branch that swept the outer grass
Far from the silver pillar of the bole
Which mounting past the house's crusted roof
Split into massy limbs, crossed boughs, a maze
Of close-compacted intercontorted staffs
Bowered in foliage where through the sun

Shot sudden showers of light or crystal spars
Or wavered in a green and vitreous flood.
And all the while in faint and fainter tones
Scarce audible on deepened evening's hush
He framed his curious and last request
For 'lime, a sprig of lime.' Her trembling hand
Closed his loose fingers on the awkward stem
Covered above with gentle heart-shaped leaves
And under dangling, pale as honey-wax,
Square clusters of sweet-scented starry flowers.

She laid his bent arm back upon his breast,
Then watched above white knuckles clenched in prayer.

He never moved. Only at last his eyes
Opened, then brightened in such avid gaze
She feared the coma mastered him again…
But no; strange sobs rose chuckling in his throat,
A stranger ecstasy suffused the flesh
Of that just mask so sun-dried, gouged and old
Which few — too few! — had loved, too many feared.
'Father!' she cried; 'Father!'
He did not hear.

She knelt and kneeling drank the scent of limes,
Blown round the slow blind by a vesperal gust,
Till the room swam. So the lime-incense blew
Into her life as once it had in his,
Though how and when and with what ageless charge
Of sorrow and deep joy how could she know?

Sweet lime that often at the height of noon
Diffusing dizzy fragrance from your boughs,
Tasselled with blossoms more innumerable
Than the black bees, the uproar of whose toil
Filled your green vaults, winning such metheglyn
As clouds their sappy cells, distil, as once
Ye used, your sunniest emanations
Toward the window where a woman kneels —
She who within that room in childish hours
Lay through the lasting murmur of blanch'd noon
Behind the sultry blind, now full now flat,
Drinking anew of every odorous breath,
Supremely happy in her ignorance
Of Time that hastens hourly and of Death
Who need not haste. Scatter your fumes, O lime,
Loose from each hispid star of citron bloom,
Tangled beneath the labyrinthine boughs,
Cloud on such stinging cloud of exhalations
As reek of youth, fierce life and summer's prime,
Though hardly now shall he in that dusk room

Savour your sweetness, since the very sprig,
Profuse of blossom and of essences,
He smells not, who in a paltering hand
Clasps it laid close his peaked and gleaming face
Propped in the pillow. Breathe silent, lofty lime,
Your curfew secrets out in fervid scent
To the attendant shadows! Tinge the air
Of the midsummer night that now begins,
At an owl's oaring flight from dusk to dusk
And downward caper of the giddy bat
Hawking against the lustre of bare skies,
With something of th' unfathomable bliss
He, who lies dying there, knew once of old
In the serene trance of a summer night
When with th' abundance of his young bride's hair
Loosed on his breast he lay and dared not sleep,
Listening for the scarce motion of your boughs,
Which sighed with bliss as she with blissful sleep,
And drinking desperately each honied wave
Of perfume wafted past the ghostly blind
Knew first th' implacable and bitter sense
Of Time that hastes and Death who need not haste.
Shed your last sweetness, limes!
But now no more.
She, fruit of that night's love, she heeds you not,
Who bent, compassionate, to the dim floor
Takes up the sprig of lime and presses it
In pain against the stumbling of her heart,
Knowing, untold, he cannot need it now.

The Stranger
Never am I so alone
As when I walk among the crowd
Blurred masks of stern or grinning stone,
Unmeaning eyes and voices loud.

Gaze dares not encounter gaze,...
Humbled, I turn my head aside;
When suddenly there is a face...
Pale, subdued and grievous-eyed.

Ah, I know that visage meek,
Those trembling lips, the eyes that shine
But turn from that which they would seek
With an air piteous, divine!

There is not a line or scar,
Seal of a sorrow or disgrace,
But I know like sigils are
Burned in my heart and on my face.

Speak! O speak! Thou art the one!
But thou hast passed with sad head bowed;
And never am I so alone
As when I walk among the crowd.

The Tower

It was deep night, and over Jerusalem's low roofs
The moon floated, drifting through high vaporous woofs.
The moonlight crept and glistened silent, solemn, sweet,
Over dome and column, up empty, endless street;
In the closed, scented gardens the rose loosed from the stem
Her white showery petals; none regarded them;
The starry thicket breathed odours to the sentinel palm;
Silence possessed the city like a soul possessed by calm.

Not a spark in the warren under the giant night,
Save where in a turret's lantern beamed a grave, still light;
There in the topmost chamber a gold-eyed lamp was lit
Marvellous lamp in darkness, informing, redeeming it!
For, set in that tiny chamber, Jesus, blessed and doomed,
Spoke to the lone apostles as light to men entombed;
And spreading his hands in blesing, as one soon to be dead,
He put soft enchantment into spare wine and bread.

The hearts of the disciples were broken and full of tears,
Because their lord, the spearless, was hedgéd about with spears;
And in his face the sickness of departure had spread a gloom,
At leaving his young friends friendless.
They could not forget the tomb.
He smiled subduedly, telling, in tones soft as the voice of the dove,
The endlessness of sorrow, the eternal solace of love;
And lifting the earthly tokens, wine and sorrowful bread,
He bade them sup and remember one who lived and was dead.
And they could not restrain their weeping.
But one rose up to depart,
Having weakness and hate of weakness raging within his heart,
And bowed to the robed assembly whose eyes gleamed wet in the light.
Judas arose and departed: night went out to the night.

Then Jesus lifted his voice like a fountain in an ocean of tears,
And comforted his disciples and calmed and allayed their fears.
But Judas wound down the turret, creeping from floor to floor,
And would fly; but one leaning, weeping, barred him beside the door.
And he knew her by her ruddy garment and two yet-watching men:
Mary of Seven Evils, Mary Magdalen.
And he was frighted at her. She sighed: ' I dreamed him dead.
We sell the body for silver. . . . '
Then Judas cried out and fled
Forth into the night! . . . The moon had begun to set:

A drear, deft wind went sifting, setting the dust afret;
Into the heart of the city Judas ran on and prayed
To stern Jehovah lest his deed make him afraid.

Thus Jesus discoursed, and was silent, sitting upright, and soon
Past the casement behind him slanted the sinking moon;
And, rising for Olivet, all stared, between love and dread,
Seeing the torrid moon a ruddy halo behind his head.

Three Songs Of The Enigma

I - Something

How long I have wished for something I know well,
But what that something is I cannot tell.

So often at sunrise in sad tears I wake
Shivering with longing for its sake;

So often at noontide when the house is still
It sickens me with its unbidden ill;

So often at twilight it does not seem far,
Not further than the first and far-off star;

All, all my life is built towards its token
Yet by its near far-offness I am broken.

For I am ever under something's spell,
But what that something is I cannot tell.

II - A Wandering Thing

The hopeless rain, a sigh, a shadow
Falters and drifts again, again over the meadow,
It wanders lost, drifts hither . . . thither,
It blows, it goes, it knows not whither.

A profound grief, an unknown sorrow
Wanders always my strange life thoro',
I know not ever what brings it hither,
Nor whence it comes . . . nor goes it whither.

III – Modern Love Song

Now that the evenfall is come,
And the sun fills the flaring trees
And everything is mad, lit, dumb,
And in the pauses of the breeze
A far voice seems to call me home
To haven beyond woods and leas.

I feel again how sharply stings
The spell which binds our troubled dust
With hint of divine frustrated things,
The Soul's deep doubt and desperate trust
That She at sunset shall find wings
To bear her beyond NOW and MUST.

So place your head against my head,
And set your lips upon my lips
That so I may be comforted,
For Ah ! the world so from me slips,
To the World-Sunset I am sped
Where Soul and Silence come to grips
And Love stands sore-astonished.

The Day's March
The battery grides and jingles,
Mile succeeds to mile;
Shaking the noonday sunshine
The guns lunge out awhile,
And then are still awhile.

We amble along the highway;
The reeking, powdery dust
Ascends and cakes our faces
With a striped, sweaty crust.

Under the still sky's violet
The heat throbs on the air …
The white road's dusty radiance
Assumes a dark glare.

With a head hot and heavy,
And eyes that cannot rest,
And a black heart burning
In a stifled breast,

I sit in the saddle,
I feel the road unroll,
And keep my senses straightened
Toward to-morrow's goal.

There, over unknown meadows
Which we must reach at last,
Day and night thunders
A black and chilly blast.

Heads forget heaviness,
Hearts forget spleen,

For by that mighty winnowing
Being is blown clean.

Light in the eyes again,
Strength in the hand,
A spirit dares, dies, forgives,
And can understand!

And, best! Love comes back again
After grief and shame,
And along the wind of death
Throws a clean flame.

The battery grides and jingles,
Mile succeeds to mile;
Suddenly battering the silence
The guns burst out awhile ...

I lift my head and smile.

Robert Nichols – A Concise Bibliography
Invocation (1915)
Ardours and Endurances (1917)
A Faun's Holiday & Poems & Phantasies (1917)
Sonnets to Aurelia (1920)
The Smile of the Sphinx (1920)
Fantastica: Being the smile of the Sphinx and other tales of imagination (1923)
Twenty Below (1926) with Jim Tully
Wings Over Europe (1928) play
Fisbo or the Looking Glass Loaned (1934) verse satire aimed at Osbert Lancaster
A Spanish Triptych (1936) poems
Such was My Singing (1942) poems

www.ingramcontent.com/pod-product-compliance
Lightning Source LLC
Chambersburg PA
CBHW070111070426
42448CB00038B/2505